D0948976

BENCHMARK BIOGRAPHIES

She Dared to Fly
BESSIE COLEMAN

by Dolores Johnson

BENCHMARK BOOKS

MARSHALL CAVENDISH
NEW YORK

Benchmark Books
Marshall Cavendish Corporation
99 White Plains Road
Tarrytown, New York 10591-9001

Library of Congress Cataloging-in-Publication Data
Johnson, Dolores.
She dared to fly : Bessie Coleman / by Dolores Johnson.
p.   cm. — (Benchmark biographies)
Includes bibliographical references and index.
Summary: A biography of the woman who became the first licensed African-American pilot.
ISBN 0-7614-0487-2
1. Coleman, Bessie, 1896–1926—Juvenile literature. 2. Afro-American women air pilots—Biography—Juvenile literature.
[1. Coleman, Bessie, 1896–1926. 2. Air pilots. 3. Afro-Americans—Biography. 4. Women—Biography.] I. Title. II. Series.
TL540.C646J63   1997   629. 13'092—dc20   [B]   96-2404   CIP   AC

Printed in Hong Kong

Photo research by Sheila Buff

Photo Credits.
Front and back cover courtesy of Arthur W. Freeman; pages 6, 12, 19, 20, 23, 29: ©Arthur W. Freeman;
pages 27, 32, 35: ©Smithsonian Institution, Negative 72-1009, 80-2384, 93-16054; page 33: The Bettmann Archive;
page 38: courtesy of State Historical Society of Wisconsin; page 48: Elizabeth King

1   3   5   6   4   2

To Judith R. Whipple
my editor, who has, in many ways,
helped me achieve my goals.

CONTENTS

Introduction 6

Young Bessie 9

First Challenges 14

Training as a Stunt Flyer 21

When Bessie Was Bravest 26

Triumphant Return 31

Tragic Endings 37

Glossary 43

To Learn More About Bessie Coleman 45

Index 47

INTRODUCTION

When Orville Wright made his first flight at Kitty Hawk, North Carolina, in December 1903, Bessie Coleman was just eleven years old. If Bessie had heard about the flight, she probably accepted the news with awe, wonder, and perhaps some disbelief. Many people thought that it would take a miracle for a human being to board a machine that could fly.

"If God had wanted people to fly he would have given us wings," some scoffed.

But less then seventeen years later another miracle seemed to happen.

Bessie Coleman decided that *she* would fly an airplane.

Why she chose flying, one of the most difficult of professions, is still a point of curiosity. Bessie Coleman did not grow up around airplanes. When she decided she wanted to be a pilot she probably hadn't even driven a car or seen a plane close up. Bessie learned to fly when others said it was impossible for a women, never mind a black woman, to pilot a plane. She set a goal and decided to work very hard until she achieved it. She chose a dream she dared to live, and she made it happen.

A portrait of Bessie Coleman taken in 1921.

YOUNG BESSIE

When Bessie Coleman was born on January 26, 1892, her future could not be foreseen by her surroundings. She was born in a one-room cabin on a dirt road at the edge of the small town of Atlanta, Texas. She was wrapped in a simple cotton quilt and was laid at her mother's side on a straw-filled mattress.

When Bessie's mother, Susan, was born, she was probably born a slave. Bessie's father, George, was three quarters Choctaw Indian and, like his wife, could not read or write. Neither of them held high expectations for their pretty, copper-colored baby daughter. In fact they probably had few high hopes for any of their children because of the times in which they lived.

At the end of the 1800s life was very difficult for many African Americans, particularly in the South. Slavery had ended just a few years earlier with the passing of the Emancipation Proclamation. Yet there were still many in the South who did not feel black people should be allowed to live as equals with white people. They established a code of conduct they called Jim Crow rules. These rules denied black people the right to use the same schools, water fountains, restaurants, and hospitals, or even to sit in the same part of the bus as white people. Because African Americans were being denied good educations, and thus good jobs, many lived in terrible poverty.

In spite of the difficulties of the times, Bessie's father managed to buy a small plot of land in Waxahachie, Texas. Waxahachie, a small town thirty miles outside of Dallas, had a large cotton industry in which the whole family could work. George Coleman used his remaining savings to build a three-room house in the black section of town.

When Bessie was six years old she walked four miles with her older brothers and sisters to the all-black school. It was a one-room building where all the students from grades one through eight were taught by one teacher. Often the black students had no textbooks or even pencils and paper, but Bessie did not let this stop her from being a good student. She loved school, and she was particularly god at reading and arithmetic. She especially regretted the period from mid-summer to late fall when the school was shut down so the black children could be sent out to the fields to pick cotton.

By 1900 Bessie's oldest sisters, Lillah and Alberta, and her oldest brother, Walter, had left the family home. Bessie's parents showed the six other children left at home plenty of love and affection, and Bessie's childhood was relatively happy. While her father did not make much money by working odd jobs as a day laborer, he still made enough to provide for his family.

But in 1901, when Bessie's father decided to return to the Indian reservation in Oklahoma where he was raised, Bessie's world fell apart. As a part-Indian in Texas culture George Coleman felt he was often treated as a savage. As a part-African American he felt he was being treated as less than a man. George wanted his whole family to move back to the reservation with him, but his wife refused.

Shortly after George left the oldest children still living at home, John and Isaiah, left as well. This meant that Susan, at age forty-five, was left alone to care for her four youngest children.

They were all girls, and one of them was Bessie.

To make a living Susan picked cotton, took in laundry, and got a job as a cook and housekeeper for a white couple. The Coleman family was very lucky because this couple provided most of the food they ate as well as much of the hand-me-down clothing they wore. The new circumstances, however, meant that Bessie had to play a larger role in helping the family make a living. Not only did she have to work in the cotton fields with her sisters, but she also worked as a bookkeeper for the other field workers. When the workers went to town to collect their pay they took smart Bessie with them so they wouldn't be cheated.

A very religious woman Susan Coleman insisted that her children go to

Bessie Coleman cut a stylish figure in her military-like uniform. Here she poses with an unidentified friend.

church. She was also a practical woman who wanted them to be well educated. Even though she could barely make ends meet she often bought books for her children from the "wagon library," which came to Waxahachie twice a year. Bessie entertained her family every night by reading the Bible, as well as books about African-American heroes like Paul Lawrence Dunbar and Harriet Tubman.

Bessie saw the role great black heroes played in America and imagined that she would play a great role herself. She felt her future was limitless. She felt she could learn anything and she would "amount to something."

FIRST CHALLENGES

Bessie finished all eight grades of school, and she longed to learn more. Some accounts of her life say she later went on to high school; others say she only finished the eighth grade. Either way Bessie desperately wanted to go to college. Her mother told her she could use her share of the money she earned washing laundry to further her education.

Doing laundry in the time before electric washing machines and dryers was hard work. Bessie started the week with a five-mile walk to pick up the laundry. She often felt embarrassed standing at the back doors of her white employers, collecting their dirty clothing. First she boiled the clothing in a large tub in her backyard, perspiration pouring down her face as she stirred the pot with a paddle. Then she took the pot off the fire so she could scrub the laundry. After this she rinsed it, starched it, and hung it up on a clothesline to dry. She pressed the laundry with an iron heated on top of a wood-burning stove. At the end of the week she walked the five miles again to deliver the clean clothes. But Bessie didn't mind the hard work because she knew it was a way to raise money to achieve her goal—going to college.

In 1910 Bessie took her savings and left home to enroll at the Colored Agricultural and Normal University in Langston, Oklahoma. Unfortunately Bessie had to drop out after completing only one term because she had run out of money. She had been such a popular student, however, that the school band went home with her to perform at her welcome-home party.

Bessie had to work as a laundress again. But in 1915 when she was twenty-three she wrote to her thirty-five-year-old brother, Walter, in Chicago and asked him for help to get out of Waxahachie. He told her she could stay with him while she looked for work. She lived in Chicago in Walter's apartment with his wife, Willie, Bessie's brother John, and John's wife, Elizabeth. Walter worked as a Pullman porter, an attendant on the railroad cars. He was the main breadwinner for all five adults.

Bessie started looking for work as soon as she got to the city. If she had stayed in Texas her only job opportunities would have been working in the cotton fields or as a laundress. In Chicago most jobs available for black women were as cleaning or factory workers. But Bessie decided she would follow another path. She took manicuring and beautician courses and got a job as a manicurist at the White Sox Barber Shop. This was an unusual career for a young black woman, but Bessie was not an ordinary person.

A black girl from a small town, like Bessie, was usually married and raising young children by age eighteen or so. Bessie did get married in 1917, when she was twenty-five, to a man named Claude Glenn. But this seemed to be a marriage of friendship rather than love. Glenn, a friend of her brother Walter, was fourteen years older than Bessie. Hardly anyone in the family even knew about the marriage. Bessie had her own apartment by this time, but the couple did not live in it together. It seems Bessie cared more about her career than in making a life with Claude Glenn.

Shortly after the wedding Bessie's mother and many of her sisters arrived in Chicago and stayed with either her or Walter. Around this same time the United States declared war on Germany, and Bessie's brothers, Walter and John, were sent to France to fight.

When they came back, John, in a teasing mood, said something to Bessie that would change her life forever. He told her that French women were better and more independent than Chicago women. They had careers—some even flew airplanes. Bessie was giving a manicure at the barbershop when John gave her this challenge, but his taunt seemed to open her eyes as well as her world. It was at that moment that Bessie decided that she would be a pilot.

"That's it!" she said. "You just called it for me."

Perhaps this daring spirit is what makes Bessie Coleman so interesting.

Before that day in the barbershop Bessie had seen pictures of planes and even read about female aviators. But she did not know much about flying. As she had done since her childhood she chose a goal and then she applied her energies to achieve it.

First she sought a way to learn to fly. She found that getting flying lessons was impossible because the white aviators and schools refused to train her—both because she was black and because she was female.

Bessie went to see Robert Abbott, publisher of the black newspaper the *Chicago Defender*. Robert Abbott was very well loved and respected by black people both in Chicago and throughout the South. He often wrote in his newspaper about how black people could better their lives, even if it meant moving out of the South. Mr. Abbott was so influential that in some southern communities it was against the law for a black person to be seen reading the *Chicago Defender.*

Robert Abbott told Bessie she needed to go to France. The French were the leaders in aviation, and Abbott felt they were not racists. He told her she must work hard, save her money, and learn to speak French. Then she could go to aviation school in France.

This was another challenge for Bessie, but she was used to challenges. Bessie knew that she lived in a country at a time that believed a woman, particularly a black woman, was incapable of piloting a plane. She was only twenty-eight years old, and she was being told she could never be more than a laundress or a manicurist. Yet she felt she could do whatever she dared to do, even if it meant going to a foreign country to achieve her goals. So Bessie enrolled in a language school and then found a better-paying job as the manager of a chili parlor. She began to save her money and then applied for an American passport. On November 20, with financial backing from Robert Abbott and a banker named Jesse Binga, she sailed for France.

Even in France Bessie ran into obstacles. When she tried to enroll in flight school, the owners of the school refused her admission. Two women had recently died while taking aviation classes with them. Again Bessie would not accept this setback.

She enrolled in a seven-month flying course at another school. There she was taught to fly, as well as to do some limited stunts. Even though she had to walk nine miles to class every day and she barely spoke French, in 1921 Bessie successfully finished the course. When she passed the test she was the first African American in the world qualified to fly. When she arrived in New York City, black newspaper reporters were waiting at the dock to celebrate the woman they called "Queen Bess."

*The Nieuport plane in which
Bessie learned to fly. She
became so impressed by it,
she tried to buy one and bring
it back to the United States.
Because of her race and her
sex, she was not allowed to
buy a plane in America.*

Bessie Coleman's aviation license. It was the first ever received by an African American. Note that her birth year is listed as 1896. Was Bessie really born four years later than was commonly believed or was she just trying to appear younger?

TRAINING AS A STUNT FLYER

Even with all the celebration when she returned to America, Bessie realized it would be very difficult for her to make a living as an aviator. Airplanes, less than twenty years after the Wright Brothers' successful flight, were little more than metal canoes with cloth-covered wings held together with wires. When Bessie stepped into one of the two cramped seats of the cockpit and flew the plane into the clouds, wind, rain, and oil from the engine would wash over her face. The plane itself would shake, roll, and lurch as it flew. The noise of the engine and the slap of the propeller would rumble in her ears.

She had few instruments to guide her and no way to talk to anyone on the ground. The ride was bumpy and the landing was worse because brakes hadn't yet been invented. But Bessie loved it.

She said, "Do you know you have never lived until you have flown?"

It was not easy for her to get a job in aviation. Up until this time almost all pilots flew planes only during wars. There were no flights across country for paying customers. The only way a pilot could make money at that time was delivering mail for the Post Office, making promotional advertising flights for businesses, or performing in airshows for the paying public.

Bessie chose the last route, probably because it was her only option. Because she was black and female she could get no other job in aviation. Her race and sex also prevented her from buying a plane.

The pilot in an airshow was called a *barnstormer.* These flying circuses moved from town to town and performed before crowds gathered on large fields rented from local farmers. The pilots got their name barnstormer because entertainers who came to rural towns to perform often slept overnight in nearby barns after performing. At the risk of their lives the pilots demonstrated aerial acrobatics like loop-the-loops (circular dives where the plane revolved in the air like the script letter *e*), stalls (stopping the engine in midair), barrel rolls (rolling over and over like a barrel), and dives.

Because of the tremendous skill needed to perform such difficult stunts, Bessie knew that with only seven months of training it would be hard for her to make a living. So in February, 1922, she sailed back to Europe to study with pilots in France, Germany, and Holland.

It was at this point in her life that Bessie Coleman began to publicly discuss another important goal. In talks before the black community she often spoke of her desire to start a school of aviation

Bessie Coleman with one of her flying instructors, Robert Thelen.
Here they are standing in a field at Aldershof, near Berlin, Germany.

where students of all races and both sexes could learn to fly. When she went back to Europe she talked to Anthony H. G. Fokker, who was known as "The Flying Dutchman" for his reputation as an aviator. She asked Fokker to come to the United States to set up an aviation school for all races. But he did not.

When Bessie sailed back to the United States she was delighted to be met at the docks by both black and white reporters. As a performer Bessie knew how important it was to create a memorable image with the press. She knew the more the press got interested in her, the more likely they were to write about her in their newspapers. With more publicity more people would come to her airshows to watch her fly and become interested in flying for themselves.

She also knew that newspapermen and their readers were most interested in colorful, exciting personalities (like Roscoe Turner, the great speed pilot who wore a lion-tamer's costume and flew accompanied by a lion cub in the second cockpit). Therefore when Bessie talked to the press she sometimes exaggerated her accomplishments or her age (which is probably why there is some confusion about her birth year). Most of the press, including some white newspaper people, were tremendously impressed by this attractive young woman who became the first licensed African American pilot.

Robert Abbott of the *Chicago Defender* asked his staff to arrange an air show for Bessie. They billed her as "the world's greatest woman flyer." The flight was scheduled for August 27, 1922, at Glenn

Curtiss Field in Garden City, Long Island. But it rained that day, and the show was delayed to September 3. When she finally did fly she made the first public flight of a black woman in America. Bessie cut quite a glamorous figure in her tailored uniform, aviator cap, boots, and leather coat.

Bessie took great care to design her uniforms as well as her total appearance. She wanted to show aviation as an attractive and adventurous profession. She was able to encourage many young people to seek a career in aviation.

WHEN BESSIE WAS BRAVEST

During the early days of aviation there were all kinds of accidents. Planes fell out of the sky and crashed for many reasons. Sometimes it was the failure of the pilot. Sometimes it was the failure of the plane. The great airshows of Bessie's day were like auto races today. Danger was always present. Pilots were risking their lives every time they started their engines.

But the threat of the loss of her life did not stop Bessie. She returned to Chicago and scheduled air shows in and around that area. She performed the most exciting stunts such as climbs, glides, and figure eights for the thousands who gathered to watch her. After the show the spectators were so excited about flying that many of them would line up to take rides on her airplane. And many young black people would approach Bessie about learning to fly.

Some African American newspapers began to celebrate Bessie as the greatest woman flyer—ever. But there were some who spoke negatively about Bessie simply because she was a woman. There were still people—some of them black, some of them women—who didn't believe a woman should be flying. Some felt that a woman would needlessly panic and could not make quick decisions in emergencies; at the least they would become upset if their clothes or faces got dirty!

Bessie Coleman was in a long line of women aviators who proved these critics wrong. Harriet Quimby, the first American woman to get a pilot's license (in 1911), was told that it would be impossible for a woman to fly across the English Channel. One man offered to dress in her clothes, fly her plane across the Channel, exchange clothes with her, and allow her to take credit. Miss Quimby did not take his offer and

COMPLIMENTS OF
MISS HARRIET QUIMBY

Harriet Quimby, the first woman awarded a flying license, was one of Bessie's first role models.

made the flight successfully on her own.

Ruth Law was an expert stunt pilot who broke and established many flight records. She offered her services as a pilot to the United States during World War I and was terribly disappointed when she was refused. Women were not allowed to fly aircraft for the American military until World War II.

Blanche Scott's flying instructor was so opposed to women flying that he put a block on her plane's throttle lever so she couldn't get off the ground. She learned to be a pilot despite these obstacles and, in 1911, was one of the first women to get her license. She became a successful exhibition flyer.

One of Bessie Coleman's foremost ambitions was to start a school of aviation where she could teach anyone who wanted to learn how to fly. But she had no money for the school, the plane, or even the hangar where the plane could be stored. She studied the career of Amelia Earhart, America's best-known female aviator of the time. Miss Earhart made her living by performing in flying exhibitions that gathered audiences. Then companies would try to sell or promote their products to the people who had gathered.

Bessie approached the Coast Tire and Rubber Company of Oakland, California. She offered to drop advertising materials for the company in exchange for a plane. They agreed and Bessie fulfilled her contract by dropping their materials over California cities.

With her new plane Bessie planned an exhibition for February 4, 1923 to cele-

*This is the plane that Bessie Coleman bought to fly an exhibition at Palomar Park
near Los Angeles in 1923. It was called a Curtiss JN-4 or "Jenny."*

brate the opening of a new fairground at Palomar Park near Los Angeles. Ten thousand people gathered to see her perform. But moments after she took off from an airport in Santa Monica for the fairground, her motor stalled and her new plane crashed. When the airfield workers ran to the demolished plane they found that Bessie had a broken leg, three fractured ribs, multiple facial cuts, and possible internal injuries.

As badly injured as she was Bessie begged her doctor to patch her up enough to get to Palomar Park. She did not want to disappoint her fans. But there was no way the doctor could get her flying again that day. She had to be placed in a cast from her ankle to her hip. She had stitches and multiple injuries. And worse, she had lost her most important material possession—her "Jenny" aircraft.

Strangely enough there were many spectators who thought that because the pilot had not appeared at the fairground, she had run away with their money. They were demanding a refund. From her hospital bed Bessie sent a telegram that read, "Tell them all that as soon as I can walk I'm going to fly.!"

TRIUMPHANT RETURN

Bessie knew she could not wait until she recovered from her injuries before she should begin raising funds again. She was thirty-one years old and she needed money for living and medical expenses. She needed to replace her plane. And she was determined to build her aviation school. So she placed an ad in a newspaper to get students for what she called "The Coleman School of Aeronautics." Tuition was to be $400. Unfortunately not enough students enrolled to get her school established.

It took three months before Bessie recovered enough to leave the hospital. She returned to Chicago in June of 1923 and worked very hard to build her barnstorming career again. She borrowed a plane and flew in an airshow on September 9 in Columbus, Ohio. Ten thousand people came to watch her. "Daredevil Erwin" also performed by hanging from his teeth from a strap suspended beneath an airplane. Iona McCarthy did triple parachute leaps and tried to land on the wings of another

After World War I, planes lilke these flying in formation had limited use in a peacetime economy.
Many surplus war planes were sold cheaply as scrap or converted for use in stunt flying.

Stunts became an important draw for airshow audiences. Stunt people performed such daring tricks as walking on an airplane's wing in flight, transferring from plane to plane in flight, and even transferring by ladder from a moving car to a flying plane.

airplane while both planes were flying.

Bessie returned to Texas, and in June of 1925 made a flight in Houston before thousands of spectators. She flew a borrowed plane high up into the clouds and stalled her motor. Then, to the relief of the crowd, she pulled the plane out of its dive a few feet before it hit the ground. She also made the plane roll over and over in a barrel roll. She did figure eights in the air and loop-the-loops. The show was so successful Bessie was signed to do three more.

In August she appeared in a show in San Antonio and had a local African American parachutist, Eliza Dilworth, jump from her plane. While doing stunt flying was very difficult, being a parachutist during the early age of aviation was really dangerous. Parachutes were packed in large canvas bags about two feet square. The bags were tied to the plane with a rope, not attached to the jumper like today's parachutes. To jump the chutist had to leave the cockpit while the plane was up in the air and walk to where the chute was tied. The jumpers attached the parachute to themselves. Then he or she would sit on the edge of the wing and jump off. With hope the jumper's weight would break the rope that held the parachute in the canvas bag. Even though Eliza Dilworth had jumped before, it took a great deal of persuading for Bessie to get her to jump for her in San Antonio. The crowd applauded wildly when she landed.

Bessie scheduled two more shows on September 5 and 6. On the fifth she asked the parachutist to jump with her.

Bessie standing in front of a Model T car as well as near her plane, a Curtis "Jenny", the "Model T" aircraft of its time.

But Eliza Dilworth refused. So Bessie sent a telegram asking for another pilot to join her. On the sixth Bessie finished her stunt flying performance and then gave the other pilot control of the plane. At three thousand feet (915 meters) she climbed out of the plane and strapped on the parachute harness. Then she walked out on the wing and jumped off the airplane. The parachute opened and she fell into the center of the crowd to instant jubilation.

This was one of Bessie Coleman's happiest summers. The crowds adored her. The press supported her. And she flew without crashing.

TRAGIC ENDINGS

Often, while criss-crossing the country on tour, Bessie Coleman spoke in churches, schools, and theaters—anywhere she could talk about flying and raise money for her flying school. As was the custom, particularly in the South, she was invited to stay at private black homes since there were few hotels where black travelers could rent a room. There were many who befriended Bessie, not only because it was the custom or because they admired her stunt-flying heroics. The supported her because she used her influence to try to end racial discrimination.

For example, in 1925, Bessie scheduled an airshow which was to be her triumphant return to her childhood home of Waxahachie. When she found that the audience was going to be segregated with the white people entering at one gate and the black people at another, she refused to perform. Finally the promoters gave in and everyone was allowed to enter by the same gate.

The next year, while in Orlando,

African American newspapers proudly claimed Bessie as a heroine and often trumpeted her accomplishments.

The Savannah Tribune.

VOLUME XLI.   SAVANNAH, GEORGIA, THURSDAY,   JANUARY 7, 1926   NUMBER 15

N. A. A. C. P. Reports Most Successful Year In History

New York, Dec. 31—The National Association for the Advancement of Colored people, today issued a summary of its Annual Report for the year 1925, showing the most successful effort in the entire history of the Association. The summary stresses the fact that segregation has been made a national issue confronting the entire American people, and that colored people through out the United States have been united in this fight as to no other except the fight to end lynching.

The N. A. A. C. P. report deals with the following subjects: 1. Segregation; 2. The "White Primary" fight in Texas and other cases of Discrimination; 3. Legal Defense; 4. Reintroduction of a revised Dyer Anti-Lynching bill in Congress; 5. Release of 24th Infantry men; 6. Publicity and Branch Organization; 7. Ku Klux Klan and Miscellaneous.

1. Segregation. During the year the N. A. A. C. P. met the issue of residential and other segregation, believing it to be perhaps the most important issue with which colored Americans have to deal. Accordingly a segregation case arising in Washington, where white property owners covenanted not to sell nor permit sale of their property to colored people has been carried before the U. S. Supreme Court where it will be argued early in January. Another case, arising in Louisiana, was also be carried before the Supreme Court and cases have been fought in the following cities:—Los Angeles and Oakland, California; Denver, Baltimore, Detroit, St. Louis, Brooklyn, N. Y., Staten Island, N. Y., (where Seamel A. Browne, engaged in business, was backed up in standing his ground against efforts to oust him from his home and in tever suing his white neighbors for $100,000); Cleveland, Pittsburgh, Fall Church, Roanoke and Norfolk, Va. In Cleveland, by court action the Board of Education of Shaker Heights was compelled to abandon the extension of colored children from their school. School cases were fought in

(Continued on Page 2)

Tales From Florida

Washington, D. C., Dec. 31—Investors, laborers, and artisans of the race, who have given Florida the "once over" during the past few months bring back a variety of tales. In the land grabbing and money-making activities, it is claimed that not a few Negroes have made small fortunes within a week or two, by the skillful turnover of Florida properties now available at high prices, only.

Negro labor is now said to be having its day in Florida, with four and five dollars a day the minimum price for the most menial work. Sixty cents per hour is said to be a low price for just fair services, or for carting men and chore help, while domestic help is said to be enjoying the height of high wages. The Seaboard and Atlantic Coast lines are bringing the full quota of Negroes each day into Florida cities, where they expect ready employment.

Notwithstanding the availability of competent Negro labor, however, it is intimated that a few promoters are still endeavoring to export labor from nearby islands, to the exclusion of American labor, and asked by this means, not a few returning Florida migrants report that even in the face of high wages the majority of Florida cities are unattractive to the Negro because of a continuance of the customs of oppression, found in Florida here and there. Said one returning migrant: "If they'd only give us a square deal all along with good doctor facilities and dancing, colonge ours without restrictions, there would be no great exodus."

WINS $150 PRIZE FOR MOST COTTON

Little Rock, Ark., Jan 6 (ANP)— James Ferguson, a share-cropper on the farm of John W. Naylor, has just been informed that he has won the $150 prize offered by the First City Chamber of Commerce for the largest amount of lint cotton gathered from five acres in St. Francis County. Ferguson yield was 4,963 pounds.

NEGRO COMPANY PLANS BIG ENTERPRISE

LOSES LIFE OVER CHITTERLINGS

Nashville, Tenn., Jan. 6 (ANP)— Angered because Mrs. Mary Noel, 50, declared he should not have any of her chitterlings unless he paid for them, Charles Wendell, on his way to the pot with a plate in his hand, struck the old woman with the plate. She thereupon seized a smoothing iron and proceeded to lay it on him. Wendell decided and fell to the floor where he lay, breathing heavily. In the morning it was discovered he was dead. Mrs. Noel is being held on a charge of murder.

Own Lawyer Wins His Case

Dunn, N. C., Jan 6 (ANP)—When Jeff Turner was accosted by a white deputy and told that it was time for him to go to bed, he resented the suggestion and an altercation ensued which resulted in the deputy taking him to jail. In court, the deputy explained that Turner had a car following in his home with the engine running and the horn blowing and that he had told him to cut out the noise. When Turner remonstrated with him, the officer said he was drunk. In Recorder's Court, Turner was his own lawyer, and told the court he had the engine of his car running to charge the battery. He conducted his case so well that he was discharged.

Another Enterprise For West Broad

New Undertaking Establishment to Open

Plans are rapidly maturing for the opening of another undertaking establishment in the city. It will have one of the finest locations on West Broad street, and in a building arranged in the latest attractive detail. The rolling stock will be of the latest style and will surpass any in the city regardless of race. Ample capital will back the enterprise and it will be composed of some of the substantial men of affairs in the city. The promoters feel that there is ample room for another enterprise of this kind and are determined to cater for public favor, giving in return service.

International Alliance Of Negroes Appoints V. D. Jenkins In Georgia

Philadelphia, Pa., Jan 6—International Alliance of Negroes, Inc. with headquarters at 1258 Lombard street, this city, has announced the appointment of V. D. Jenkins who will to give sanction to perform the program of work throughout Georgia, especially in the southeastern portion of the State. Dr. Jenkins is widely known, especially throughout the South, where he has been for a number of years engaged in church and ministerial work. He is also field Agent as General Supervisor for the State of Georgia, of the Joint Committee to promote helpful relations between the Republic of the United States and the Republic of Liberia. He is at present located at 124 Crumley street, Atlanta, Ga.

Dr. And Mrs. Sweet And W. White On Speaking Tour

Dr. and Mrs. Ossian H. Sweet, released on bail pending retrial of their case in Detroit and Walter White, Assistant Secretary of the National Association for the Advancement of Colored People, are to deliver addresses in five large cities, to stimulate interest in the Legal Defense Fund being raised by the N. A. A. C. P.

Meetings have been arranged by N. A. A. C. P. and cooperating groups, as follows: Jan. 5, Philadelphia; 6, Baltimore; 7, Washington in the Metropolitan A. M. E. church under the auspices of the colored women of Washington; 8, Pittsburgh, and Jan. 10, Cleveland. Retrial will not begin in early January as originally planned. Date for opening of the second trial has not yet been fixed by the Court.

EMANCIPATION CELEBRATION WAS GENERALLY OBSERVED

But Few Organizations In The Procession—Rev. E. W. Rakestraw Delivers Forceful Address—Church Packed to the Gallery

With ideal weather prevailing, early Friday morning January first, West Broad street, was a scene of activity, as many persons busied themselves in preparation for the celebration of Emancipation day.

Men and women in uniform were going to and fro and decorated automobiles were dashing from one side of the city to the other. This was a day on which Savannah Negroes were celebrating the sixty-third anniversary of the issuance of the Emancipation Proclamation.

The celebration was under the auspices of the Social Club Union which is composed of many of the social organizations of the city and the Emancipation Association which comprises the ministers. The celebration was begun by a street parade in the morning ending with appropriate exercises at St. Philip A. M. E. Church, Charles and West Broad street which was packed.

The parade moved off from West Broad and Henry streets ate 11:30 o'clock and wended its way through the principal streets of the city. The procession fell short of the marchers that have paraded in previous years and not of the large number of social clubs in the city only two were inline marching. they were the Savannah Home Association and the Young Adelphians. The streets were thronged with people to witness the parade which was headed by chief marshal, Capt Julius Maxwell who was aided by Robert Roddom and C. W. Herns as assistant marshals.

Following the marshall, Middleton's band the Staff officers of the Uniform Rank Knights of Pythias headed by Col. M. W Bryan, immediately behind the staff was a lone walker carrying a United States Flag which is the sole survivor of the Robert Shaw Post of the Grand Army of the Republic.

Then came the fire company of the Knights of Pythias and the Columbia Drill Corps and Boy Scouts, which made up the first division.

The second division was headed by the Elks Band and staff officers of the Uniform Bank Knights of Pythias with Col. Robert Johnson in command and four companies. In this division was also uniformed department of the American Woodmen, the Girl Scouts, Medion Lodge of Elks, Savannah Home Association and the Young Adelphia Club.

The third division of the parade was made up of automobiles, headed by several cars conveying the officers of the Emancipation Association and several Club's Union, the speaker of the day, the master of ceremonies and the

(Continued on Page 2)

REV. E. W. RAKESTRAW
Principal Speaker at Emancipation Celebration

FORMER BOSSES BACK ACCUSED

New York, Jan 6 (ANP)—Although police claim to have found one of James Garces $124 which Margaret Burton, a white waitress, said he had stolen from her pocket booked in a restaurant, two former assistant secretaries of the United States Treasury, Jarett Souspe and Edward Clifford, have asked that the case be investigated because of their belief in James honesty. They claim he was employed as a guard in the treasury department while they were in office and that he often had the opportunities to be dishonest, but never was. His record was without a blemish. He is under indictment on a charge of grand larceny.

DARING COLORED FEMALE AVIATRIX

She Is The Only Colored Authorized Flier in The Country

The city was thrilled by the visit of Miss Bessie Coleman, the well known colored aviatrix, who appeared during the week at one of the local theatres and who will exhibit her skill in the aviation fields on Sunday, if conditions for same are fully met.

A young lady with unlimited confidence in herself. She is a Texas, having being born in Atlanta of that state. In 1919 she went to France to take up flying after being refused in this country. She met with success. She is regularly licensed by the French government, and has held some since 1921. She is the only accredited colored flier in this country, and her main anxiety is to see the number increased She owns her own airplane, which is in Texas and would appear in same if sufficient inducement was offered.

She left for Augusta, where she has an engagement, but will return Saturday in order to appear in exhibition Sunday at the Daffin Park fields. On this occasion she will walk the wings of the airplane and do other stunts.

Dr. Alexander Reports Mississippi Roused Over Lynching

In a letter to James Weldon Johnson, Secretary of the National Association for the Advancement of Colored People, Dr. W. W. Alexander, Director of the Commission on Interracial Cooperation in Atlanta, reports that the State of Mississippi is aroused over the recent lynching of Lindsay Coleman, a Negro, immediately after he had been acquitted of a charge of murder by a jury in Clarksdale.

Dr. Alexander writes that "reports indicate that the State is aroused as never before. The Governor is determined and, I think, has sufficient support to write a new chapter in Mississippi history. You may be quite sure that we will keep as much pressure on the situation as possible.

"The Governor of Mississippi has very little authority. In fact, none except the power to call out the militia. He, with the support of the Bar Association, and other influences of Mississippi, will ask the legislature at its opening session to empower the Governor to remove sheriffs and give him quite sure that we will keep as much his authority that will enable him to bring real pressure on lob local economically. I think such legislation has a good chance of passing.

The campaign of education will go on in Mississippi, Mrs Henderson of my staff will spend most of the month of January going from community to community in the State speaking and organizing the women effectively against mob action. Mr. Hanner, of my staff, will go into all the colleges and many of the high schools for the same purpose."

Dr. Alexander's letter was written in response to a communication from the N. A. A. C. P. asking what the people of the State intended to do about the latest lynching in view of the strong pronouncement recently made by the Bar Association of Mississippi against mob violence and mob murder.

WOULD RATHER BE A SLAVE

Goldsboro, N. C., Jan 6 (ANP) The oldest person in this city is James Allen, who was born Dec. '15, 1800, is therefor going into his 117th year. He was born a slave and owned by a man who had about 150 slaves. In an interview with a reporter for a local daily the old man expressed great regret that the old slavery days are gone, explaining "I'd rather be back like I was then when I had three square meals a day and somebody to look after me than like I am now. When I used to get sick the white folks would send old Doctor Faison to look after me, and now when I get sick I have to do the best I can."

The exercises at the church were begun by the address of Rev. E. W. Rakestraw, pastor of Asbury M. E. Church who did credit to himself and to the occasion. For about three quarters of an hour he presented a beautiful flow of oratory that held the large audience spell-bound which was broken only by the frequent rounds of applause. It was a forceful address and one of the ablest delivered on a similar occasion for a number of years.

The address of Rev. Rakestraw appears in full as follows:

"Master of Ceremonies, Comrades in the "Gospel of Christ, fellow citizens:

"Providential intervention has removed this crude and honorable responsibility upon me.

"The short space of time in which I

(Continued on Page 2)

Gives Away Pot Of Gold

New York, Jan 6 (ANP)—The Word of this city gives to interesting story of Samson Harper a second ex-service man who struggled through seven years of poverty to partial success and now has decided to donate what he gained to the aid of other unfortunate ex-soldiers. Harper returned from the war physically impaired and without funds for a start in life. He surmounted obstacles of a kind, working hundreds of miles, sleeping under, subway steps and lying off crusts to educate himself at various technical schools. For six years pretty bad and then there was a turning point. Last year The World paid for a telegram he sent to President Coolidge. From this time on things seemed to get better and Harper was recently awarded an adjusted service certificate, valued at $1,221. Now he proposes t give this as the basis of a fund which will enable other youths regardless of race or religion, to get an education. He, hopes his example will lead other veterans to make a similar use of their bonus awards.

STEAL YEAR'S SAVINGS FROM AGED WOMAN

Woodbury, N. J., Jan 6 (ANP)— Police are looking for two young men who flim flamed an aged colored woman out of $85, all as possessed of a year's savings. She is Mrs. Anna Wicks, 79 years old, of 34 Nelson Avenue, this little town.

Evidently the flim-flammers knew the woman had a little money. When she left her home Christmas Eve three ncgroes she was met by one of the men, who inquired about a street in town. He walked beside her as the second fellow approached. This latter suddenly stooped and picked up a pocketbook, apparently bulging with money. Then he assumed the role of friend to the other men.

"I'll tell you what we'll do," said the first. "Since we are all in on the find, we will divide itup, but let's go what where we have."

While it was a ridiculous proposition, Mrs. Wicks agreed, went home, obtained the $85, and accompanied them to Camden, 12 miles away, where one of the men desired to visit the office of his employer. They arrived in Camden, but just where Mrs Wicks doesn't know, then one of the men took her money and they both also produced some bills. Apparently they counted out a very large sum. One said it was $2,200 and that each would get a third.

Mrs. Wicks with visions of unexpected wealth, readily accepted a pocket

CONGRESS STUDIES LABOR MEASURES

Washington, D. C., Jan 6 (ANP)— According to Robert L. Mays, president of the Railway Men's International Benevolent Industrial Association, which has headquarters in Chicago, two bills have recently been introduced in congress of importance to the 150,00 colored railroad workers in the United States. The bills were placed before the house of representatives by Congressman Martin B. Madden, Republican from Chicago.

One of the measures would affect the creation of a labor board subsidiary to the United States Railroad Labor Board and would be known the Federal Railroad Adjustment Board. This board would be expected to consider all cases, involving points at issue between employers and employees which would be assigned to it by the Railroad Labor Board. The decisions of the proposed board in order to be valid would have to be approved by the Railroad Labor Board which would also have the power of amendment or rejection. Its action would be final. The Federal Railroad Adjustment Board would be composed of six members, appointed under the same conditions and terms as members of the existing board, and compensation would be at the rate of $8,000 a year for each member. An effort is being made to have one Negro appointed in this board. This personage is the most important of Assistant United States Attorney General Clarence Matthews.

The other measure introduced by Mr. Madden would nullify provisions in existing or future contracts which restricted or in any way interfered with the right of a railroad company to employ any person in any capacity and make, lawful only such rules and work ing conditions as applied to all employers alike, whether they are members of unions or not.

18 LYNCHINGS IN 1925 GAIN OVER LAST YEAR

Florida, Bessie was booked to do a parachute jump. She threatened to cancel her performance when she heard that black people would not be allowed to attend. The white Chamber of Commerce backed down, and Bessie successfully performed. The *Chicago Defender* wrote that Bessie probably lost substantial sums of money during her career because she refused any flying engagements which did not allow African Americans in the audience.

Yet Bessie could not break down all racial barriers. When she tried to buy a plane with money she had managed to save, she found they would not sell a plane to an African American in Florida. Later she went to Dallas, Texas, where she put a down payment on a reconditioned plane called a Curtiss "Jenny." But

they wouldn't let her take it off the lot until she paid in full.

Bessie finally found an investor who gave her the money needed to pay off the remaining debt. She took a train to Jacksonville, where she had been scheduled to lecture, directing a white mechanic named William D. Wills to fly the plane to her. The plane was an old one, and the twenty-four-year-old mechanic had problems with it. The plane twice had engine trouble, forcing William Wills to make five, rather than three landings during the twenty-one-hour flight. When he finally arrived in Jacksonville the other pilots at the airfield were surprised that he was able to get the worn old engine all the way to Florida.

On Saturday, May 1, 1926, Bessie was scheduled to perform in a May Day air show for the Negro Welfare League. She was thrilled that a well-respected organization like the league was giving her support. On the day before the performance Bessie knelt in prayer by the side of her plane and then climbed into the rear cockpit while Wills, the mechanic, took the controls. She wanted to sit in the back and let him pilot the plane so that she could study the airfield for the next day's jump.

At first Wills piloted the plane in graceful patterns. But then the soaring circles became wild and out of control, and the plane suddenly nose-dived to the ground. Bessie, who was not strapped in by her seat belt, fell out of the plane to her death, breaking every bone in her body. Wills struggled with the plane and seemed to regain control.

But he hit a pine tree and crashed to the ground as well.

A bystander foolishly lit a cigarette near the crash, igniting the gas fumes and setting the plane on fire. Later investigators found that someone had left a wrench inside the engine, jamming the gears.

The loss of Bessie Coleman, the first black female aviator, was felt so deeply that she was given three funerals. In Jacksonville, white, black, rich, and poor filed past her coffin for hours.

After another funeral service in Orlando, Bessie Coleman's body was flown to Chicago. There ten thousand people tried to attend the funeral. She was buried at Lincoln Cemetery in southwest Chicago on May 7, 1926.

In the thirty-four short years of Bessie

Coleman's life, she struggled against many odds. Yet she never stopped working, with great determination, to fulfill her goals. She was know as "Queen Bess" or "Brave Bessie" for her stunts in the air.

But those were not the accomplishments that made her royal or brave. It is because she dared to chose a goal that was virtually impossible to achieve, and in almost every attempt she achieved it. It is because Bessie Coleman dared to fly that countless people—black and white, young and old, women and men—can dare to dream their dreams and achieve them.

Glossary

Aerial: Having to do with airplanes and air.

Aeronautics: The science of flying.

Airshow: A performance of stunt pilots, wingwalkers, parachutists, etc., or air races over an audience usually standing in a large field.

Aviation: The science of flying an airplane.

Aviator: The pilot of an airplane.

Barnstormer: A pilot in an airshow, or performers like wingwalkers or parachutists who perform stunts.

Barrel Rolls: The stunt in which the plane rolls over and over in the air like a barrel.

Beautician: A person who works in a beauty parlor and whose primary job is to style hair.

Emancipation Proclamation: The document Abraham Lincoln signed on January 1, 1863, that freed all slaves in territories that were in rebellion with the Union.

Flying Circuses: Airshows.

Jim Crow Rules: A series of rules used to discriminate against African Americans.

Hangar: Large building at an airport where airplanes can be housed.

Laundress: A person who washes laundry for a living.

Loop-the-loop: Circular dive in which the plane revolves in the air like the script letter *e*.

Manicurist: A person, usually a woman, who treats hand and fingernails in a beauty shop.

Parachute: A large umbrellalike cloth device that allows a person to descend slowly to the ground after jumping from an airplane.

Parachutist: A person who jumps from an airplane and uses a parachute to land safely. Also called a "chutist."

Stall: When the engine of a plane stops either as part of a stunt or as mechanical failure.

To Learn More About Bessie Coleman

Boyne, Walter J. *The Smithsonian Book of Flight*. Washington, D.C., New York: Orion Books, 1987.

Casey, Gerry A. *Flying as It Was: True Stories from Aviation's Past*. Blue Ridge Summit, PA: Tab Books, Inc., 1987.

Dwiggins, Don. *Famous Flyers and the Ships They Flew*. New York: Grosset & Dunlap, 1969.

Freydberg, Elizabeth Amelia H. *Bessie Coleman, the Brown Skin Ladybird*. New York: Garland Publishing, 1994.

Hardesty, Von, and Pisano, Dominick. *Black Wings: The American Black in Aviation*. Washington, D.C.: National Air and Space Museum, Smithsonian Institution, 1983.

Harris, Sherwood. *The First to Fly: Aviation's Pioneer Days*. New York: Simon and Schuster, 1970.

King, Anita. "Brave Bessie: First Black Pilot, Parts I & II." *Essence* Magazine: May and June 1976.

Lomax, Judy. *Women of the Air*. New York: Dodd Mead, & Co., 1986/87.

May, Julian. *Amelia Earhart: Pioneer of Aviation.* Mankato, MN: Creative Educational Society, 1973.

Rich, Doris L. *Queen Bess, Daredevil Aviator.* Washington & London: Smithsonian Institution Press, 1993.

Roberts, Evangeline. *Chicago Pays Parting Tribute to "Brave Bessie Coleman."* Chicago: *Chicago Defender,* May 8, 1926, p.1.

Sachs, Robert. Letter. *California Eagle,* March 4, 1923, p. 4.

Smith, Jessie Carney. *Notable Black American Women.* Detroit, London: Gale Research, Inc., 1992.

Tessendorf, K. C. *Barnstormers & Daredevils.* New York: Atheneum, 1988.

African American Biography, Volume 1. Detroit: Gale Research, 1994.

"They Take to the Sky," *Ebony* Magazine, May 1977.

Index

Page numbers for illustrations are in boldface.

Abbott, Robert, 17, 18, 24
African Americans
   African American heroes, 13
   African American parachutist, 34, 36
   black newspapers, 17, 18, 24, 26, 27, **38**, 39
   discrimination against, 9-10
airplanes
   biplane, **33**
   Curtiss JN-4 ("Jenny"), **29**, 30, **35**, 39
   World War I, **32**

barnstormers, 22
Binga, Jesse, 18

Chicago Defender, 17, 24, 39
Chicago, Illinois, 15-16, 40
Coast Tire and Rubber Company, 28
Coleman, Alberta (sister), 10

Coleman, Bessie, **7**, **12**, **19**, **20**, **23**, **25**, **35**
air shows, 24-25, 26, 31, 34, 36, 37, 39
aviation license, **20**
buys first plane, 39
childhood, 9-11, 13
death, 40
decision to become a pilot, 6, 16
desire to start aviation school, 22, 24, 28, 31, 37
first flying exhibition, 28-30
as first licensed African American pilot, 24-25
flying lessons, 17-18
injuries, 30
as laundress, 14-15
as manicurist, 15-16
marriage, 16
"Queen Bess", 18, 41
stunt flyer training, 21-22

stunt flying, 26, 28, 31, 34, 36
Coleman, Elizabeth (sister-in-law), 15
Coleman, George (father), 9, 10, 11
Coleman, Isaiah (brother), 11
Coleman, John (brother), 11, 15, 16
Coleman, Lillah (sister), 10
Coleman, Susan (mother), 9, 11, 13
Coleman, Walter (brother), 10, 15, 16
Coleman, Willie (sister-in-law), 15
Colored Agricultural and Normal University, 15

"Daredevil Erwin", 31
Dilworth, Eliza, 34, 36
Dunbar, Paul Lawrence, 13

Earhart, Amelia, 28
Emancipation Proclamation, 9

Fokker, Anthony H. G. ("The
    Flying Dutchman"), 24

Glenn, Claude, 16

Jacksonville, Florida, 40
Jim Crow rules, 10

Law, Ruth, 28

Lincoln Cemetery, Chicago, 40

McCarthy, Iona, 31

Negro Welfare League, 40

Orlando, Florida, 37, 39, 40

Quimby, Harriet, **27**

Savannah Tribune, The, **38**
Scott, Blanche, 28

slavery, 9
stunt pilot, **33**

Thelen, Robert, **23**
Tubman, Harriet, 13
Turner, Roscoe, 24

Waxahachie, Texas, 10, 13, 37
Wills, William D., 39, 40
World War I, 16
    airplanes, **32**
Wright, Orville, 7

ABOUT THE AUTHOR

Dolores Johnson was born and raised in New Britain, Connecticut, and is a graduate of Boston University. She is the author-illustrator of seven picture books for children: *What Will Mommy Do When I'm at School? What Kind of Babysitter Is This? The Best Bug to Be, Your Dad Was Just Like You; Now Let Me Fly: The Story of a Slave Family; Seminole Diary,* and *Papa's Stories.*

In addition to writing and illustrating books, Ms. Johnson teaches writing at a community college. She lives in Inglewood, California.